30
Biography Book Reports

Easy and Engaging Hands-On Literature Response Projects that Help Kids of All Learning Styles Explore the Genre of Biography

by Deborah Rovin-Murphy

SCHOLASTIC
PROFESSIONAL BOOKS

New York • Toronto • London • Auckland • Sydney
Mexico City • New Delhi • Hong Kong • Buenos Aires

To my wonderful, supportive husband Frank—
and my two little history makers, Griffin and Chase.

Acknowledgements:
Thank you to Morgan Waldinger for her amazing projects—
and to Mr. Kelly's class for all of their hard work!

Cover design by **Josué Castilleja**
Interior design by **Holly Grundon**
Interior illustrations by **Mona Mark**

ISBN # 0-439-21570-6
Copyright © 2001 by Deborah Rovin-Murphy
All rights reserved.
Printed in the U.S.A.

Contents

Activities

Introduction

Why Use Biographies?

Biographies are a link to our past. They bring history to life: Readers can feel, taste, and see history through the life of the person who lived it. The biography subject becomes a reader's tour guide to another time. A biography of a person who achieved his or her goals, through hard work, determination, and ambition can also serve as a student's inspiration and a role model.

A biography can teach both problem solving and how to overcome obstacles. Students can empathize with the real problems of notable people. Biographies are a genre that students can enjoy and learn from for the rest of their lives!

The activities in this book help students experience the stories of remarkable people who were once very much like themselves. By making a Venn diagram, writing a newspaper article, creating math word problems, giving speeches, and much more, students will explore the lives of their heroes and discover what they may have in common with them. Your class will write, explore, solve problems, and create while learning about history.

How to Use This Book

The activities in this book can be used with individuals, small groups, or the whole class, and can be used with any biography. Students might select the activities they wish to complete.

Getting Started

Introduce your biography unit by making a variety of biographies available in your classroom. Include a wide variety of subjects, both men and women, representatives of different ethnic groups, and people from different time periods. Make sure your collection provides books at various reading levels and includes a variety of formats, such as picture books, autobiographies, and anthologies.

Helping Students Select a Biography

When helping a student select a biography, keep in mind their interests and reading ability. For instance, depending on reading level, you might help students select a picture book, easy reader, short chapter book, or novel. Student interests might include sports (Peggy Fleming, Tiger Woods), writing (Gary Soto, Emily Dickinson), adventure (Lewis and Clark, Sally Ride), and so on.

Possible Biographical Subjects

☆ U.S. presidents
☆ World explorers
☆ Astronauts
☆ Musicians
☆ Writers
☆ Business leaders
☆ Scientists
☆ Activists
☆ World leaders
☆ Entertainers
☆ Philosophers
☆ Artists
☆ Athletes
☆ Inventors
☆ Pioneers

Introductory

Create Interest

Discuss what makes a person notable. Ask students to brainstorm a list of notable people on a sheet of paper. Record students' suggestions on chart paper. Categorize their suggestions (athletes, writers, and so on) and post the list as a class reference.

Guess and Match

From the biographies you have available in your classroom or library, select five subjects' names and write them on the board. Then make a list of their occupations or accomplishments. Let students match each person to his or her accomplishment.

Example

1. Charles Lindbergh   a. astronaut
2. Wilma Rudolph   b. baseball player
3. Neil Armstrong   c. pilot
4. Marie Curie   d. Olympic medalist
5. Babe Ruth   e. scientist

Activities

Biography Bop

1 To help students select who they might read about, play this fun variation of musical chairs. Have each student stand behind a desk with chairs pushed in, waiting until the music starts. When the music begins, students begin walking around the room. When the music stops, students sit at the closest desk.

2 Students open the biography on their desks and quietly skim the book for approximately 3-5 minutes until the music begins again. Continue the game for several rounds.

3 When finished, let each student share information about the people they read about during the game.

Materials

a different
biography
for each
student's desk

tape/CD player

Sincerely Yours

Write a letter to a biography subject.

1 This activity lets students envision a personal connection with their subject by asking questions and making comments. Have students list two or three questions they would like to ask their subject. For example, "Dr. Seuss, how did you feel when your first book was rejected twenty three times?"

2 Have students list two or three interesting facts about the subject. Then, have them list one of the subject's accomplishments and one important event that occurred during his or her life.

3 Using the questions and information they've written down, students can write a friendly letter to the subject on Reproducible 1. Model how to write facts in such a way that it sounds like a friendly letter. For example, "It must have been exciting to be one of the first people to walk on the moon!"

Materials

Reproducible 1
page 32
(one per student)

pens/pencils

ms. mae Jemison

Dear Diary

Write an imaginary diary entry.

1 Have students pick an important event in the life of the subject. (For example, Jackie Robinson's first day with the Dodgers or the day the Wright brothers flew at Kitty Hawk.)

2 Ask students to think about how the person may have felt on this special day. Have them write diary entries on Reproducible 2, including facts they know to be true as well as their own speculations. (For example, "Today I took off in my Electra plane in an attempt to fly around the world. I'm both excited and a little bit nervous. —Amelia Earhart")

3 Have students complete several diary entries from different times in the subject's life.

Materials

Reproducible 2
page 33
(*one or more
per student*)

pens/pencils

Extra! Extra!

Write a newspaper article.

1 Discuss with students the six questions reporters ask when covering a story (Who? What? When? Where? Why? How?). Bring in local newspapers for students to examine as examples of newspaper-style writing. Have students pick an important event in their subject's life.

2 On the first line of Reproducible 3, students each write a creative headline related to an event in their subject's life. For example, "Kid Genius Composes Symphony" for Wolfgang Amadeus Mozart.

3 Using facts from the biography, students write and illustrate a news article under the headline.

Materials

Reproducible 3
page 34
(one per student)

drawing supplies

pens/pencils

Tip

As a prewriting activity, have students write "reporter's questions" down one side of a sheet of paper. They can then jot down answers on the other side of the page, using information from the biography.

Activity 4

Those Were the Days

Make "snapshots" for a biography subject's photo album.

1 Discuss how photo albums or scrapbooks hold memories and pictures of important events (if possible, share a photo album or scrapbook as an example). Tell students to close their eyes and imagine that they have entered their biography subject's house and are exploring their surroundings. (For example, if they are in Thomas Edison's house, they might see a phonograph, paper with ideas written on it, or an electric light bulb.)

2 Have students list three important events from their subjects' lives. They can look back through the biographies for ideas.

3 Distribute three index cards to each student. Invite students to draw a "snapshot" of each event they listed.

4 After completing the drawings, students put photo corners on the index cards and attach them to a sheet of construction paper. They might add captions. Assemble the scrapbook pages into a class biography scrapbook!

Materials

index cards
(three per student)

photo corners

construction
paper

drawing supplies

pens/pencils

Historical Problem Solving

Incorporate math into the study of a biography subject.

Materials

pens/pencils
paper

1 Discuss with students the idea that math is everywhere: Thomas Edison held over 1,000 patents. Galileo's telescope could make objects appear 1,000 times larger and 30 times closer than as seen with the naked eye. Babe Ruth had a record of 714 home runs when he retired! Invite students to brainstorm five number-related facts about their subject.

2 Students use the facts to write math problems. Use the following as examples:

Fact: Betsy Ross was one of 17 children.
Math Problem: If Betsy Ross was the eighth child born, how many children were older than Betsy? How many were younger?

Fact: Harry Houdini often gave 20 shows a day.
Math Problem: If Harry Houdini gave 20 shows a day, how many shows would he give in 5 days?

3 When students finish writing their math problems, they can trade with partners to solve.

Tip

Copy students' problems and put them in a center for independent math work.

Activity 6

Wish Book

**Create a wish book using the
character traits of biography subjects.**

1 Explain that one reason we read biographies is because we
admire certain traits or attributes that the subject possesses.

2 Have students name people studied in class and write each
person's name down. Beside each name, students write one
character trait they admire in that person.

For example:

Shakespeare   creativity

Thomas Edison   many interests

Wilma Rudolph   persistence

3 Then, students complete a
wish book using their lists.

For example:

I wish...

I were as creative as Shakespeare.

I had as many interests as Thomas Edison.

I had persistence like Wilma Rudolph.

4 To make the book, students fold a stack of sheets of paper in
half and staple along the fold. They decorate the cover and
use each page for one "wish."

Materials

drawing paper

drawing supplies

pens/pencils

stapler

Biography Poems

Try three different types of poetry.

1 Write an Acrostic Poem

Have students write the subject's first and last name in all capital letters vertically on a piece of paper. They can then use each letter as the beginning of a word or phrase that relates to that person.

For example:

Abe Lincoln

Avid reader
Brave
Emancipation

Log cabin
Indiana and Illinois
Noteworthy president
Civil War
Open to new ideas
Lawyer
Non-discriminating

2 Write a Clerihew Poem

A clerihew is a poem written about a famous person. It is four lines long and consists of two rhyming couplets.

For example:

Abe Lincoln

Abe Lincoln was a great president.
You can see him on a shiny, copper cent.

He helped the United States end slavery.
He is known for his honesty and bravery.

3 Write a Diamante Poem

A diamante poem is shaped like a diamond, and uses the following formula.

Line 1	person's first name
Line 2	two words that describe the person
Line 3	three "–ing" words related to the person
Line 4	four related nouns
Line 5	three words that describe how the person felt or things they did
Line 6	two more describing words
Line 7	person's last name

For example:

George
wise, brave
fighting, leading, thinking
general, president, farmer, leader
planned, commanded, planted
kind, humble
Washington

Hero Trading Cards

Create fun-fact hero trading cards.

1 Using Reproducible 4, have students draw a portrait of their biography subject and label it with his or her name.

2 Have students add facts they learned from their reading.

3 When complete, they cut the sheet in half and mount back-to-back on colorful construction paper (trim the paper around the card). Students can trade their cards and have fun learning about each other's biography subjects.

Materials

Reproducible 4
page 35
(one per student)
construction paper
glue
drawing supplies
pens/pencils

Tip

Put cards in a filing box for students to use as a reference.

Hanging Out With History

Create a visual representation mobile.

Materials

hanger

white paper

yarn

markers

crayons

hole puncher

index cards

tape

scissors

1 Students identify four important facts related to their subject and think of an image or picture that represents each fact.

2 Students create and cut out four pictorial representations. They punch a hole in each and attach them with yarn to a coat hanger, and label each picture with the fact about the subject.

3 Write the name of the subject on an index card and tape it to the inside of the hanger. Display mobiles from the ceiling.

Bookmarks

Make bookmarks to teach other readers about a biography subject.

1 Explain that just as advertisers come up with catchy phrases to promote their products, students can promote their subject by making biography bookmarks. Have each student divide a sheet of paper into four rectangular sections using a ruler, and cut them out.

2 Students write a catchy phrase related to their subject on one side of the bookmark. They can decorate the bookmark with a picture of their subject or a symbol. On the other side of the bookmark, students write three related facts about their subject.

3 Each student can make four different bookmarks on their subject(s). After the bookmarks are complete, punch a hole in the top and attach a tassel made of yarn. Make a grab bag and let students select two bookmarks made by their classmates!

Materials

thick white paper
hole punch
yarn
ruler
drawing supplies
pens/pencils
scissors

Alike and Different

Discover what you have in common with a biography subject.

1 Draw a Venn diagram on the board.

2 As an example, select two volunteers to compare and contrast themselves. Ask about their hobbies, likes and dislikes, interests, and dreams. Write things that the two students have in common in the overlapping part of the circles. Write their differences in the appropriate circles.

3 Invite students to brainstorm what they have in common with their biography subject and how are they different. Students can then complete their own Venn diagram.

Materials

Reproducible 5
page 36
(*one per student*)

pens/pencils

Postcards From the Past

Put yourself in the role of a subject in order to reply to postcards.

Materials

index cards or postcards

shoebox

drawing and decorating supplies

pens/pencils

1 Create a class mailbox from a shoebox and explain that it is a magical mailbox because it can deliver letters to the past. On the mailbox or chalkboard, display a list of biography subjects that students are studying. Place blank index cards or postcards by the box.

2 Invite students to write postcards to one of the subjects from the list, asking questions about their life.

3 Check the mailbox to see which subjects have mail. Students who have read about that subject can then write a response to the postcard from the subject's point of view.

Packed With History

Fill a biography subject's suitcase.

Materials

small, clean pizza boxes

construction paper

art materials

found objects

1 Distribute one pizza box to each student. Have students cover their boxes with brown construction paper and attach a cardboard handle to one end of the box to make a suitcase. They might attach a luggage tag with the biography subject's name on it.

2 Inside each suitcase, students place items (made from art materials or collected from home) that relate to their biography subject.

My Character's Character

Analyze a subject's character traits.

1 Review the concept of character traits with students (explain that they are a person's special identifying qualities).

2 Have each student make a list of their biography subject's character traits. Let them choose four traits and write them on the top line of each section of the reproducible.

3 Students draw a picture of their subject in the center of the reproducible. Underneath each character trait, students give examples. For example, for Rosa Parks a student might choose "Courageous" and write "She was courageous for standing up for what she believed in and not giving up her seat."

Medal of Honor

Focus on one accomplishment that represents a subject.

1 Discuss how each subject has something that makes his or her contribution to the world unique. Using the reproducible, students write the name of the person being honored at the top of the medal.

2 They list what the subject is being honored for. For example, Martin Luther King for courage; Michelangelo for creativity.

3 Students can color and cut out the medals for a class display.

Materials

Reproducible 6
page 37
(one per student)

pens/pencils

Materials

Reproducible 7
page 38
(one per student)

crayons or markers

scissors

pens/pencils

Materials

Reproducible 8
page 39
(*one per student*)

pens/pencils

Jumping Hurdles

Describe how a subject overcame an obstacle or solved a problem.

1 Point out that hard work and perseverance are needed to reach a goal.

2 Using Reproducible 8, students list, on the left side, a problem or obstacle that arose in their subject's life. On the right side of the hurdle, students write how the subject solved the problem.

3 Then, on the bottom of the page, students do the same for an obstacle or problem in their own lives.

Materials

Reproducible 9
page 40
(*one per student*)

pens/pencils

Report Card

Evaluate a subject's performance.

1 Explain to the class that just as teachers complete report cards by giving a grade and an evaluation, they can do the same with their subjects.

2 Tell students to imagine that they are each the teacher and their student is their biography subject.

3 Have students fill out Reproducible 9 by giving their biography subject a letter grade for each school "subject" and writing their comments.

A Life at a Glance

Make a time line of a subject's life.

1 Starting with the subject's birth, have students list at least five important dates in their subject's life. The time line ends with either the subject's death or the present year.

2 Help students mark off increments of time on a sentence strip to make a time line. They record each important event on the time line.

3 Students illustrate the important events on their time lines.

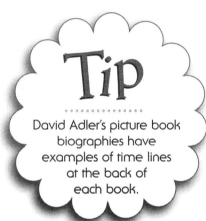

Tip

David Adler's picture book biographies have examples of time lines at the back of each book.

Materials

sentence strips
drawing supplies
pens/pencils

Try a Group Time Line, Too:

Using information from individual time lines, create a class time line.

1 Cut butcher paper in half lengthwise to make a long, narrow sheet of paper.

2 Survey the class to find the subject with the earliest birth date. Construct the time line, using this date as the beginning point and the present date as an ending point. Students plot the birth dates on the time line and add pictures.

Materials

long sheet of butcher paper
drawing supplies
pens/pencils

Materials

map of the world

paper

drawing supplies

double-sided tape

scissors

Mapping It Out

Create an origin map.

1 Point out that notable people come from places all over the world. Display a large world map.

2 Have students draw, cut out, and label a small portrait of their subject.

3 Students can stick the portraits of each subject's place of origin on the map with double-sided tape.

Materials

Reproducible 10
page 41
(one per student)

pens/pencils

scissors

glue

paper

Guess Who?

Write clues for others to guess the subject.

1 On Reproducible 10, students fill in information from their research as clues to the identity of their biography subject. Students reveal the time period, a symbol that represents the subject, a quote, and an action that is identified with the subject. Remind students not to make clues too easy or too difficult.

2 Students make a portrait of the subject on a piece of paper the size of the question mark square at the bottom right of the sheet. Then, they cut out three sides of the question mark square to make a flap and glue the portrait behind the flap.

3 Partners exchange papers and try to guess each other's subjects.

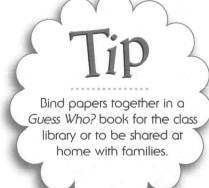

Tip

· · · · · · · · · · ·

Bind papers together in a *Guess Who?* book for the class library or to be shared at home with families.

Graph It

Conduct a class survey and graph the results.

Materials

paper
drawing supplies

1 Discuss the variety of biography subjects students are reading about. List the following categories on the board:

● female subjects

● male subjects

● subject still alive

● subject not living

2 Survey students and put tally marks in the appropriate categories. You might also use categories about the time period in which the subject lived, countries of origin, and so on.

3 Using the information obtained in the survey, students create pie graphs or bar graphs.

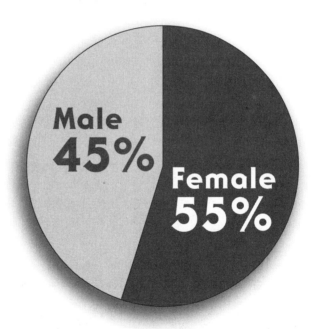

Male 45%

Female 55%

Situation Wanted

Write an ad for the classifieds.

Materials

paper
pens/pencils

1 Show students the classified ads from newspapers in your area. Explain that a "want ad" is placed by an employer looking to hire someone to work for them, and a "situation wanted" ad is placed by a person trying to find a job.

2 Have each student write a "situation wanted" ad by listing the special skills of his or her subject. For example:

"Looking for work. Good with words and witty sayings. Good speaker. Experience with a printing press. Willing to travel. Will take risks. Please contact Benjamin Franklin, Philadelphia, Pennsylvania."

Tip

Use a computer to set students' ads in columns like the want ads section of a newspaper.

Get Into Character

Present a dramatic oral report by "stepping into the shoes" of a subject.

1 Students draw the head and torso of their subject on a large sheet of poster-board, leaving a hole where the person's face would be, and add accessories. For example, a "feather pen" in Ben Franklin's hand. Extras may include clothing, pictures, and other props.

2 Students present oral reports in the persona of the subject while sticking their heads through the hole in the cut-out.

Laura
Ingalls Wilder

Materials

posterboard
scissors
drawing supplies
found objects

Filmstrip Fun

Make a filmstrip of scenes from a subject's life.

Materials

Reproducible 11
page 42
(one per student)

cube-shaped
tissue box
(one per student)

wrapping or
construction paper

drawing supplies

scissors

1 Have students cut the tops off square tissue boxes. Then, they wrap the box in wrapping or construction paper, leaving the cut side open.

2 Students cut slits opposite each other on two sides of the box, for pulling the filmstrip through.

3 On the reproducible, students draw four scenes from the life of their subject in chronological order.

4 Students cut out the filmstrips and pull them through the slits as they narrate the biography.

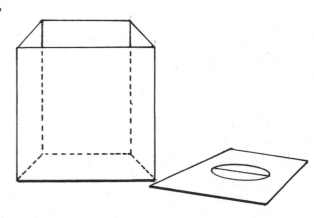

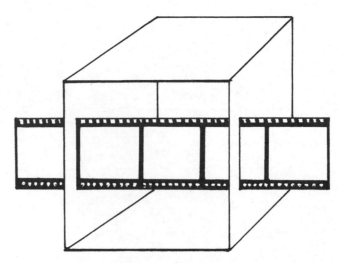

Our Collections

Honor a subject with a commemorative stamp and coin.

1 Show students stamps and coins of famous persons. Have students write why they think their subject should be featured on a stamp or coin.

2 Using Reproducible 12, have students design a stamp and coin honoring their subject. Encourage students to try to incorporate details about what makes this person notable into the picture. For example, for Neil Armstrong, show a rocket or the moon in the background.

3 Display the finished products on a bulletin board titled "Our Collections."

Materials

Reproducible 12
page 43
(one per student)

drawing supplies

WOMEN IN MEDICINE

Elizabeth Blackwell

CIVIL RIGHTS HERO

Rosa Parks

Biography Box

Decorate a cereal box with images that represent a subject's life.

Materials

empty, clean
cereal boxes
(*one per student*)

white drawing
paper

drawing supplies

scissors

glue

1 Have students outline each of the four upright sides of the cereal box onto white drawing paper and cut out the rectangles.

2 Have students make a title for the biography box on one of the large rectangles. Have them decorate the cut drawing paper with facts, a time line, illustrations, quotes, poetry, pictures, or objects related to the subject.

3 Glue the decorated sheets to the sides of the cereal box and display.

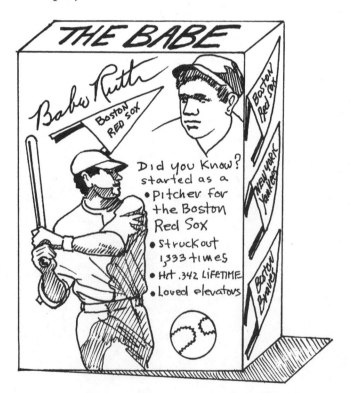

Story of My Life

Write your own autobiography.

1 Explain the meaning of the terms *biography* and *autobiography*. *Auto* means "self," *bio* means "life," and *graph* means "drawing" or "writing."

2 Instruct students to complete Reproducible 13 to help structure their writing. Have students write a draft based on their answers. Then have them revise the draft into a final paper.

3 Bind the stories into an autobiographic collection in the classroom library.

Materials

Reproducible 13
page 44
(one per student)

pens/pencils

Museum Statue

Make a clay statue of a subject.

Materials

clay

manila paper
(one 14"x14"
square per
student)

scissors

drawing supplies

stapler

1 First, let students make clay models of their biography subjects.

2 Have them make backdrops for the clay figures (see below). Fold down one corner of the manila square to form a triangle. Unfold and fold the opposite corner to form a triangle. Unfold. Cut a slit down one crease to the center. Fold one triangle made by the cut under the other and show students how this will later be stapled to form backdrop.

3 Have students decorate the backdrop (for example, Christopher Columbus might have a ship backdrop), staple and place their models into the display.

fold

cut

Encyclopedia Entry

Create a class encyclopedia of notable people.

1 Discuss how information is presented in encyclopedias (you might examine one together).

2 On Reproducible 14, students write a biographical sketch of their subject. Students draw a picture of their subject along with dates next to the paragraph entry.

3 Bind into a class book! Put your encyclopedia in the classroom library.

Materials

Reproducible 14
page 45
(one per student)

pens/pencils

Activity 30

Biography Bash

Celebrate the biography genre with a party!

At the conclusion of your biography unit, have students share what they have learned by hosting a Biography Bash. Decorate the classroom with all the projects you have created during the unit. Invite other classes, school personnel, and families to the party.

You Might:

- Encourage students to dress up as their subjects.

- Have students give their "Get Into Character" reports (see page 25).

- Give out door prizes such as biography bookmarks (page 17) and hero trading cards (page 15).

- Have students display their work on their desks. Students can answer questions as their biography subject.

- Present each student with the medal of honor for their subject.

- Display student-authored biographies and autobiographies.

- Display your encyclopedia (see above).

Sincerely Yours

_____

_____

_____

_____

Dear _____ ,

_____

_____

_____

_____

_____

_____

Sincerely Yours,

_____

Dear Diary

date _____

Dear Diary,

date _____

Dear Diary,

Biography Bugle

Extra! Extra!

_____

_____

_____

┌─────────────────────────┐   _____
│   │
│   │   _____
│   │
│   │   _____
│   │
│   │   _____
│   │
│   │   _____
│   │
│   │   _____
│   │
└─────────────────────────┘   _____

_____

_____

_____

_____

_____

Hero Trading Cards

Name: _____

Created by: _____

Heroic Facts: _____

Subject's Name:

Your Name:

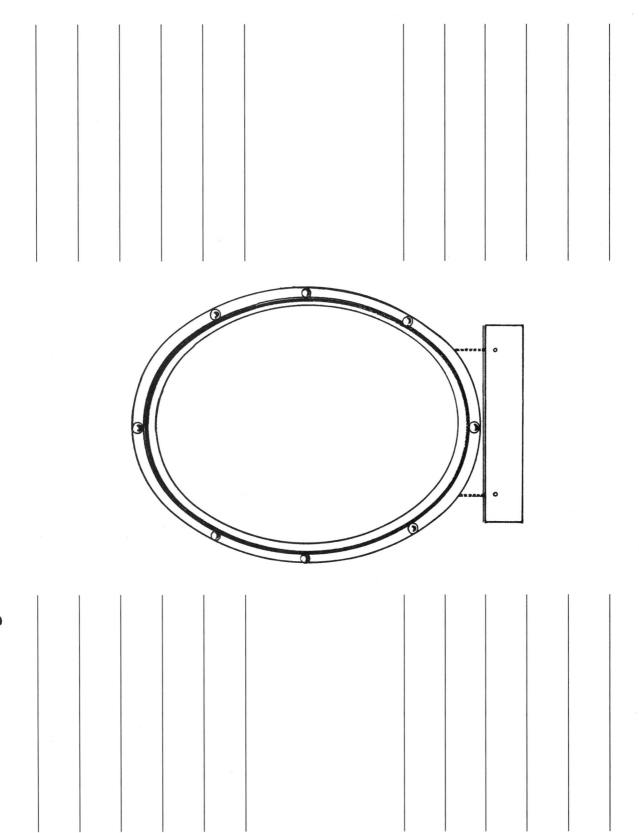

My Character's Character

Medal of Honor

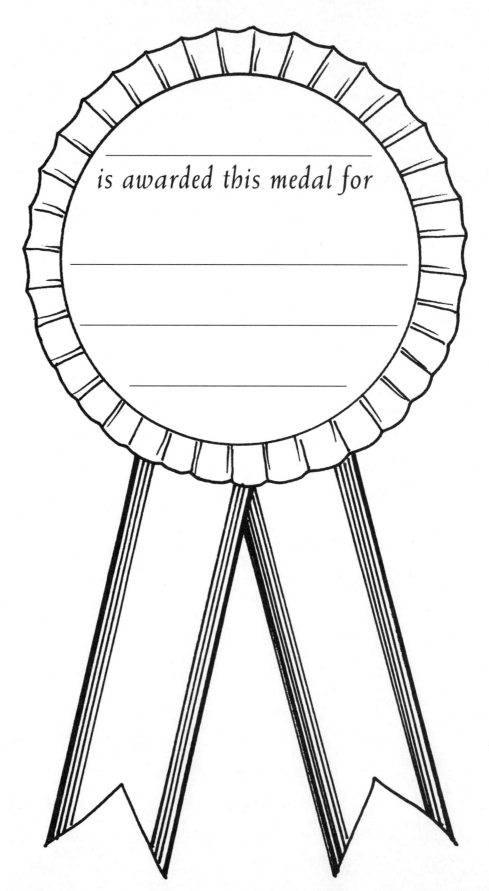

is awarded this medal for

Jumping Hurdles

Obstacle/Problem   Solution

_____   _____

_____   _____

_____   _____

_____   _____

_____   _____

_____   _____

_____   _____

Report Card

SUBJECT	GRADE

BRAVERY . . . . ☐

COMMENTS:

_____

_____

STRENGTH . . . . ☐

COMMENTS:

_____

_____

WISDOM . . . . ☐

COMMENTS:

_____

_____

RISK-TAKING . . . . ☐

COMMENTS:

_____

_____

Guess Who?

Time Period

Symbol

Quote

Action

Extra Clues

Filmstrip Fun

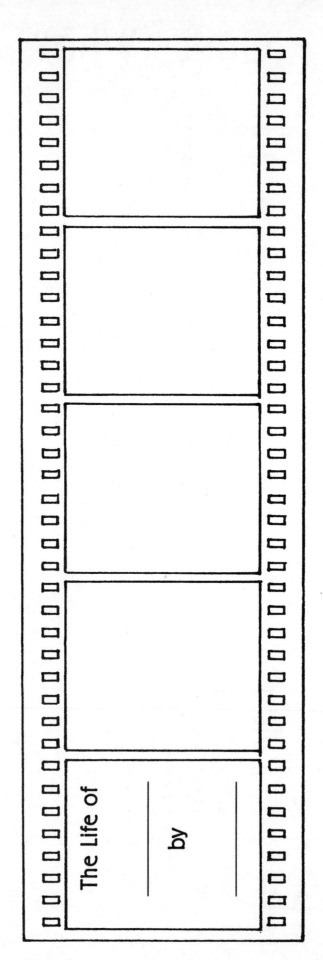

The Life of _____

by _____

Our
Collections

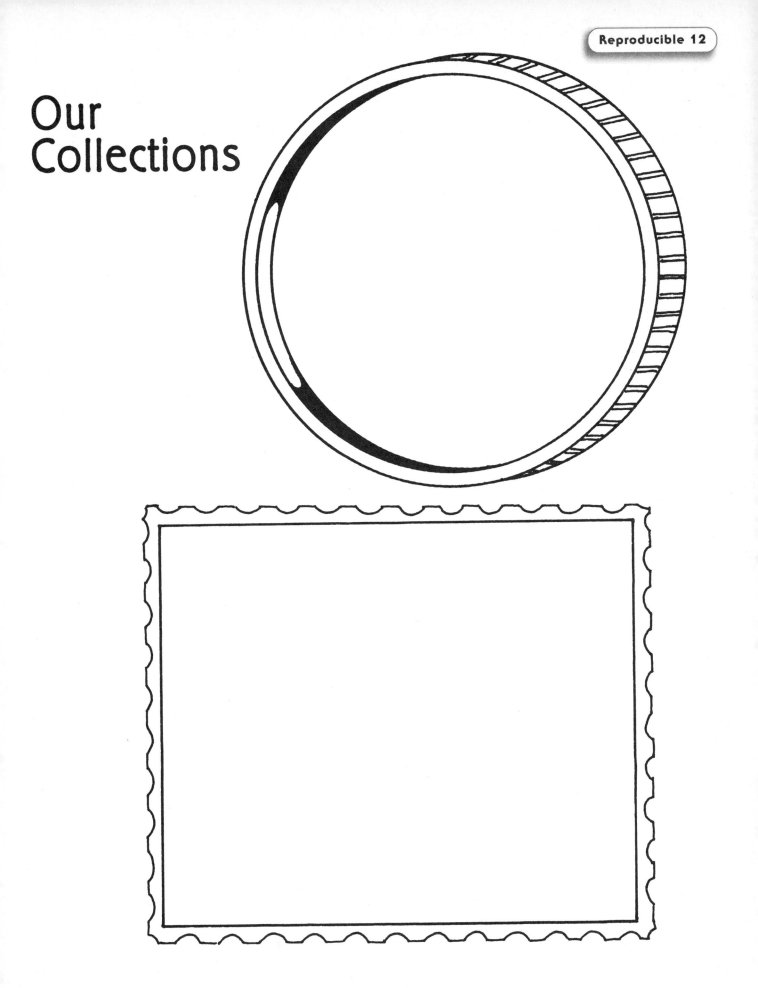

Story of My Life

Name: _____

Date of Birth: _____

Place of Birth: _____

Family members/ages: _____

_____

A memory from each year...
(ask a family member for the early years)

_____

_____

_____

_____

_____

_____

List an accomplishment you're proud of:

_____

_____

_____

What do you want to be when you grow up?

_____

_____

Encyclopedia Entry

name of subject   dates

Bibliography of Children's

Series

Step into Reading (Random House)

The Fly on the Ceiling: A Math Myth
by Julie Glass (1998)

The Great Houdini
by Monica Kulling (1999)

Abe Lincoln's Hat
by Martha Brenner (1994)

Tiger Woods: Golf's Young Master
by Sydelle A. Kramer (1998)

Step-Up Biographies (Random House)

Meet Abraham Lincoln
by Barbara Cary (1989)

Meet George Washington
by Joan Heilbroner (1989)

Hello Readers (Scholastic)

A Girl Named Helen Keller
by Margo Lundell (1995)

A Boy Named Boomer
by Boomer Esiason (1995)

Rookie Biography (Children's Press)

Elizabeth Blackwell: First Woman Doctor
by Carol Greene (1991)

Madam C.J. Walker: Pioneer Businesswoman
by Marlene Toby (1995)

Margaret Wise Brown
by Carol Greene (1994)

Childhood of Famous Americans (Aladdin)

Sitting Bull: Dakota Boy
by Augusta Stevenson (1996)

Henry Ford: Young Man With Ideas
by Hazel B. Aird (1986)

Roberto Clemente: Young Ball Player
by Montrew Dunham (1997)

Clara Barton, Founder of the American Red Cross
by Augusta Stevenson (1986)

Troll Biographies (Troll Publishing)

Young Rosa Parks: A Civil Rights Heroine
by Anne Benjamin (1996)

Young Martin Luther King, Jr.: I Have a Dream
by Joanne Mattern (1991)

Biographies

Women of Our Times (*Puffin*)

Laura Ingalls Wilder:
Growing Up in the Little House
by Patricia Reilly Giff (*1996*)

Mary McLeod Bethune: Voice of Black Hope
by Milton Meltzer (*1996*)

Our Golda: The Story of Golda Meir
by David A. Adler (*1986*)

David A. Adler's Picture Books
(*Chelsea House*)

A Picture Book of Helen Keller (*1992*)

A Picture Book of John F. Kennedy (*1999*)

A Picture Book of Paul Revere (*1995*)

A Picture Book of Simon Bolivar (*1992*)

A Picture Book of Fredrick Douglass (*1995*)

Gateway Biographies (*Millbrook Publishing*)

Bill Clinton: President of the 90s
by Robert Cwiklik (*1997*)

Colin Powell: Straight to the Top
by Rose Blue (*1997*)

Bill Gates: Computer King
by Josepha Sherman (*2000*)

Lives of... by Kathleen Krull (*Harcourt Brace*)

Lives of the Writers: Comedies, Tragedies
(And What the Neighbors Thought) (*1994*)

Lives of the Musicians: Good Times, Bad
Times (And What the Neighbors Thought) (*1993*)

Lives of the Artists: Masterpieces, Messes
(And What the Neighbors Thought) (*1995*)

Lives of the Presidents (*1998*)

Lives of the Athletes: Thrills, Spills
(And What the Neighbors Thought) (*1999*)

Notable Picture Books With Biographical Subjects

You Forgot Your Skirt, Amelia Bloomer
by Shana Corey (*Scholastic 2000*)

Young Teddy Roosevelt
by Cheryll Harness
(*National Geographic Society 1998*)

Snowflake Bentley
by Jacqueline Briggs Martin
(*Houghton Mifflin 1998*)

Leonardo Da Vinci
by Diane Stanley (*William Morrow 1996*)

Cleopatra
by Diane Stanley (*William Morrow 1994*)

Lou Gehrig: The Luckiest Man
by David A. Adler (*Gulliver 1997*)

The Babe and I
by David A. Adler (*Gulliver 1999*)

America's Champion Swimmer
by David A. Adler (*Raintree/Steck-Vaughn, 2000*)

Wilma Unlimited: How Wilma Rudolph Became the World's Fastest Woman
by Kathleen Krull (*Harcourt Brace 1996*)

Stone Girl, Bone Girl: the Story of Mary Anning
by Laurence Anholt (*Orchard 1999*)

Pioneer Girl: The Story of Laura Ingalls Wilder
by William Anderson (*HarperCollins 1998*)

What's the Big Idea, Ben Franklin?
by Jean Fritz (*Putnam 1976*)

Amelia and Eleanor Go For a Ride: Based on a True Story
by Pam Munoz Ryan (*Scholastic 1999*)

The Legend of the Teddy Bear
by Frank Murphy (*Sleeping Bear 2000*)

Steamboat! The Story of Captain Blanche Leathers
by Judith Heide Gilliland (*DK 2000*)

Tutankhamen's Gift
by Robert Sabuda (*Atheneum 1994*)

The Starry Messenger
by Peter Sis (*Farrar Straus & Giroux 1996*)

William Shakespeare and the Globe
by Aliki (*HarperCollins 2000*)

Computer Connections

The following are helpful websites for information on biographies. Teacher guidance is suggested in order to ensure appropriate website content.

http://www.s9.com/biography
This dictionary can be searched by birth years, death years, positions held, professions, literary and artistic works, achievements, and other key words.

http://www.biographiesonline.com
This website is a resource for finding books on a particular subject.

http://www.bham.wednet.edu/bio/biomaker.htm
This website lists step-by-step how to write a biography.

http://www.brainbrawl.com/lesley/biographies.htm
This website provides links to selected biographies available on the Internet.

http://www.biography.com
This site is connected with the A&E Biography television program.